Wallace Foster

# The Deaf Soldier

A brief synopsis of one hundred and two cases of deafness

Wallace Foster

**The Deaf Soldier**
*A brief synopsis of one hundred and two cases of deafness*

ISBN/EAN: 9783337175689

Printed in Europe, USA, Canada, Australia, Japan

Cover: Foto ©ninafisch / pixelio.de

More available books at **www.hansebooks.com**

# HEADQUARTERS

# Silent Army of Deaf Soldiers, Sailors and Marines,

1090 NORTH TENNESSEE STREET.

INDIANAPOLIS, IND.

*To the Senate and House of Representatives of the United States:*

In addition to the reasons and evidence we have previously submitted in behalf of Union ex-soldiers who are suffering from total and approximating total deafness, the following compilation and extracts from letters, are printed with such other memorandum as will enable the reader to comprehend readily each case.

These letters are sincere, the testimony of experience, and are deserving of consideration, inasmuch as they present features not usually made so prominent nor generally known to any except fellow sufferers. These letters are not exceptional cases chosen from a large number to represent a case different from what the whole number would indicate, but include each and every letter available for the purpose from the time their compilation was first considered up to the hour of going to press.

These men left their comfortable homes with all the love of patriotism, joyous manhood and vigorous health, having a perfect sense of hearing, and served their country faithfully and effectively.

To-day they are shut out from nearly all the gainful occupations, and so helpless as in many cases to require assistance from those who can hear to transact their business for them.

It is believed that a candid reading of the matter presented will convey a better understanding of the equity of their claims, and of the urgent necessity for the relief they deserve.

We do feel that we have not that aid from a generous government that is extended to fellow comrades who were as faithful, but have suffered less.

In this little volume are startling proofs of the sincerity and soundness of our plea, which can not be denied or ignored, as the undersigned have undergone every degree of deafness, and speak what we know of the misery it causes.

Respectfully submitted,

A. G. P. BROWN, PRESIDENT,
Capt. 24th N. Y. Cavalry, 382 Bergen St., Brooklyn, N. Y.

WALLACE FOSTER, SEC. AND TREAS.,
Capt. 13th Ind. Infantry, 1090 N. Tenn. St., Indianapolis, Ind.

## EXHIBIT 1.

R. S. H. Age 47. Waverly, New York.
A, 107th New York Infantry.

### Total Deafness of Left Ear and Severe of Right. Caused from Wounds and Disease.

"Shell wound on head at Battle of Antietam, fracturing my skull and rendering me unconscious for some time. Following my recovery from wound I was taken with typhoid fever, resulting in deafness as stated above. After my recovery and on duty again, I suffered greatly from embarrassment and chagrin on account of not being able to hear the commands of my officers while on drill and in battle. At the Battle of Chancelorsville I found myself inside the rebel lines, on account of not hearing the orders to fall back. Being very dark at the time, I fortunately escaped to our lines.

"On account of the terrible embarrassments of my deafness, and the awful adventitious sounds in my head caused thereby, I was obliged to leave my business, that of pharmacist, and finding it difficult to obtain any employment, I resumed the study of medicine, graduating after the most painful efforts to hear the lectures, many of which I could not hear at all. Making up for lost time, I had to purchase the professors' printed works and lectures, reading them at night. When I began practice, I found men of lesser advantages and ability left me far behind, many people telling me they would gladly employ me but for my deafness. Many times I have been tempted to give up in despair, but knew not what to do, as almost every avocation was closed against me, even the blind being able to procure a livelihood at more avocations than the deaf. Making a special study of deafness and its accompanying nervous disorders, I have come to consider the deaf as enjoying far less of the blessings and comforts of life than the blind, and this is corroborated by the best authority among the blind. Eye strain has come to be understood by the laity as causing poor health and innumerable nervous disorders. It is equally well known to specialists in the treatment of aural troubles that a far greater number of nervous and far greater physical suffering is produced by ear strain and inability to hear. The blind are universally cheerful, contented and even happy, while the deaf are morose, despondent and unhappy, many of them developing melancholy, and ending their days in the mad-house, while others suiciding on account of their isolated and unhappy condition, a notable instance being a professor in the New York College of New York city, who blew out his brains on account of the awful noises in his head (which every deaf person suffers from). This and the nervous disorders are, perhaps, more notable before that living death, total deafness, is reached; but when that ensues, who that has not experienced it can describe it? One of my patients who became suddenly deaf, and was as suddenly restored a few weeks later, became delirious from joy at her recovery, and came near losing her mind upon her escape from what she described as worse than death.

"There are several of the more permanent nervous troubles connected with deafness, which I will mention:

"*First.* Vertigo, which is very distressing where there is a disparity of hearing between the two ears. Tinnitus (or noises) are of varied character and intensity, being most distressing to every one who suffers from deafness. Straining to catch sounds wearies the mind and body excessively, as it is a putting forth of nature's reserve nerve force under full tension.

"Headache, hemicrania, neuralgia, loss of memory, extreme sensitiveness to loud and sharp sounds which shock the brain and nervous sensibilities, causing nervous prostration. Insomnia, or disturbed sleep, and constant dreaming, aggravated and augmented by the increased noises from which he suffers at night. Hyperaesthesia, and other deranged sensations of skin. Disturbed digestion, reverberations and echoes of harsh sounds heard for hours and days. Confusion of mental faculties when exposed to excitement and noises. Irritability of temper, numbness of feeling, despondency and feelings indescribable by pen or tongue, engendered by the fact (made evident a thousand times a day) that we are considered dumb on account of our deafness, and that we are an intolerable nuisance to those who are more fortunate. These are only a few of the sufferings of the deaf."

## EXHIBIT 2.

W. H. N. Age 55. Eldorado Springs, Missouri
A, 25th Illinois Infantry.

Totally Deaf in One Ear and Severe in the Other, with Diseased Eyes. Caused from the Explosion of a Shell at the Battle of Stone River.

"After my discharge from the service I followed my trade (plasterer), and three years ago I had to give up my trade in consequence of my growing deafness and defective sight, and am now without the means of support. I am constantly troubled with dizziness, noises in my ears like the running of saws, buzzing of bees, roaring of water, ringing of bells, sounds that I am unable to describe, and leaves me all worn out from nervous prostrations."

## EXHIBIT 3.

D. S. A. Age 71. Ottawa, Kansas.
Chaplain 1st Illinois Cavalry and 15th Illinois Infantry.

Total Deafness of Left Ear and Approximating Total of Right. Caused From Severe Cold, Resulting in Catarrh.

"Have very frequent and exceedingly unpleasant sounds, singing, roaring in my head, with dizziness and loss of memory. I was a chaplain while in the army, and a pastor before entering the service. Since my return, and owing to my increasing deafness, I have not been able to serve as a regular pastor for more than fifteen years, and am obliged to do anything that I can get to do, so as to obtain the necessaries and comforts of life. I am now receiving a pension of $22 per month, but that amount is entirely insufficient to support myself and wife in our old age. At the same time, however, I am thankful to my Heavenly Father and to the best government upon earth, which our brave and self-denying soldiers saved, for the help afforded in my declining days. I hope, by the grace of God, after a few more years shall have passed away, to enter upon a state of being, where God, my Heavenly Father, will supply my every want."

## EXHIBIT 4.

G. M. C. AGE 58. CORNING, NEW YORK.
I, 20TH CONNECTICUT INFANTRY.

TOTALLY DEAF IN LEFT EAR AND NEARLY SO IN RIGHT.
CAUSED BY BEING STRUCK ON THE LEFT SIDE OF MY HEAD BY A PIECE OF SHELL IN THE BATTLE OF PEACH TREE CREEK, GEORGIA.

"The noise in my ears is similar to roaring of the sea, or large shell held close to the ear, only louder. I am a machinist by trade, but have had to give it up several times on account of my hip. I traveled on the road for a while but had to give up my situation on account of my growing deafness. Between the two disabilities I am incapacitated from nearly all the gainful occupations, not being able to perform manual labor."

## EXHIBIT 5.

D. B. AGE 60. INDIANAPOLIS, INDIANA.
HEAVY ARTILLERY.

SEVERELY DEAF IN BOTH EARS, APPROXIMATING TOTAL.
CAUSED BY CONCUSSION FROM ARTILLERY.

"Was a merchant and postmaster in a small town, and a good part of the time had to employ some one to hear for me, until, finally, in the spring of 1887, I had to resign my commission as postmaster and sell my business, because I could not hear well enough to transact business, and could not afford to employ another to do it for me. I am crippled with rheumatism, which disqualifies me for doing but very little manual labor, and I can not find work, because I am deaf."

## EXHIBIT 6.

J. L. Age 55. Bird Island, Minnesota.
K, 2d Minnesota Infantry.

---

Severely Deaf in Both Ears.
Caused by Sickness and Too Much Quinine.

"Was a builder and in the railroad business until I was obliged to give up both on account of my hearing. I have been unable to obtain employment for the last ten years, except as farmer. I am unable to do any hard physical labor, consequently not getting one quarter the wages I received while on the railroad and builder. I suffer from ringing in the ears and dizziness. On taking a slight cold I have roaring, snapping and cracking noises that take all my strength and leave me prostrated."

## EXHIBIT 7.

---

T. J. Aged 51. Spearfish, Dakota.
20th Illinois Infantry.

---

Nearly Totally Deaf in Both Ears.
Caused by Explosion of Shell Near My Head.

"By occupation a carpenter. Can get no work at my trade because I am subject to vertigo and can not hear the orders when on a building. I have many distressing noises in my ears, like ringing of bells and escaping of steam, which confuses me so much that I am good for nothing For several years I have been unable to do any manual labor, and clerical work I can not get, on account of my deafness."

## EXHIBIT 8.

R. L. Age 45. Stanberry, Missouri.
G, 30th Iowa Volunteers.

Totally Deaf in Both Ears.
Caused by Exposure and Catarrh.

"I am wholly unable to obtain employment in any capacity on account of my total disability. My present occupation is farming, and by reason of my depleted system I can not perform any manual labor. I have roaring, cracking sounds, and rushing of blood to my head. I am never called upon to converse with any one unless they have something very special. I simply live in a world of my own, looking and expecting something that never comes, and my life is a burden."

## EXHIBIT 9.

C. H. Age 56. Preston, Wisconsin.
46th Ohio Volunteers.

---

Severe Deafness in Both Ears.
Caused by Concussion of Artillery, and Exposure.

"My former occupation was farmer. I am practically unfit to do any business or manual labor. I have a sharp, stinging sensation in my ears and can get no relief until I shake the ear."

## EXHIBIT 10.

J. F. Age 53. Red Bird, Missouri.
A, 32d Missouri Infantry.

---

Nearly Total Deafness of Both Ears.
Caused by Sunstroke.

"I have tried farming and several other occupations, and from the mistakes I made in business transactions I had to give them all up. I have dizziness and roaring, rumbling and hissing noises in my head and ears, like a swarm of a million grasshoppers, that almost sets me wild. I am in no business, for the reason that I am unable to attend to any on account of my misfortune."

## EXHIBIT 11.

---

N. S. Age 50. New Stark, Ohio.
H, 118th Ohio Infantry.

Total Deafness in Right Ear, and Nearly so in Left.
Caused by Explosion of Shell.

"I had to give up my occupation of miller on account of my defective hearing, dizziness and constant noises in my ears. Can not perform any manual labor or transact business. My lack of hearing is a great hindrance. Deprived of all pleasure and social enjoyment with my family or friends, I am doomed to live a life of my own, imprisoned from the joyful and sweet sounds of Nature."

## EXHIBIT 12.

P. W. Age 70. St. Clair City, Michigan.
Battery H, Michigan Light Artillery.

Total Deafness of Left Ear, and Severe in the Right.
Caused From Pleurisy and Catarrh.

"Former occupation a farmer, which I have not been able to follow for twelve years. Have great difficulty to speak or do any business. Am totally incapable of earning my living and have been for ten years, and all for reason of my disability."

## EXHIBIT 13.

J. C. F. Age 53. Palestine, Illinois.
D, 24th Ohio Infantry.

Severely Deaf in Both Ears.
Caused from Concussion of Artillery.

"I am by occupation a wagon-maker, but had to give up working at my trade on account of my deafness. I have tried many other kinds of work, but have been discharged on account of my misfortune. I have distressing noises in my ears; also, dizziness at times so bad that I fall prostrate. Have beside other disabilities a gun shot wound in left side."

## EXHIBIT 14.

T C. Age 54. Castleton, Vermont.
2d Vermont Light Artillery.

Totally Deaf in Right Ear, and Severely in Left.
Caused by Concussion of Artillery.

"My head gets very dizzy, and when I stoop I can not get up without having something to hold on to. There is no feeling in the right side of my head, and my sight is failing very fast. There is no noise in my right ear, which is totally deaf, but a continual noise in my left ear, like water falling. I am unable to do any kind of manual labor or any kind of business. I have not earned a cent in ten years, and half of my pension goes for doctor bills. My deafness grows worse every month."

## EXHIBIT 15.

J. M. P. Age 47. Redfield, Dakota.
McClellan Dragoon Squadron, 12th Illinois Cavalry.

Totally Deaf in one Ear and Practically so in the Other.
Caused by the Bursting of a Shell, and explosion of Ammunition Train.

"I have tried farming, but could not follow the business on account of my deafness. Since I have been deaf I have been shut out of every avenue of earning a living. I am broken down in health, and all I have to live on is my pension."

## EXHIBIT 16.

J. H. D. Age 50. New Philadelphia, Ohio.
I, 60th Indiana Infantry.

Severely Deaf in Both Ears.
Caused by Exposure and Catarrh.

"My deafness has caused me much suffering and loss of time. After leaving the army I learned telegraphing, and when they discontinued the register and operated by sound I was compelled to give up a lucrative position on account of my disability. I have tried a great variety of occupations, but was unable to fill any of them for reason of my deafness. There is no employment for me except light work around my own home."

## EXHIBIT 17.

F. C. T. Age 51. Lopez Island, Washington.
14th United States Infantry.

Totally Deaf in Right Ear, and Nearly so in Left.
Caused by Exposure and Sickness.

"I often think, which is the most valuable member of the human body—the limbs, eyes or ears? They are indeed all valuable and good members to have. I am a carpenter by trade. What contractor wants a deaf carpenter? A deaf man will only be employed when no other men can be had. This is my experience, and I find it so in all kinds of work. A deaf man has little or no show for work to earn a living."

## EXHIBIT 18.

L. G. C. AGE 49. NORTH PARSONVILLE, MAINE.
15TH VERMONT VOLUNTEERS.

TOTALLY DEAF IN LEFT EAR AND SEVERELY IN RIGHT.
CAUSED BY EXPOSURE, ETC.

"By profession I am a preacher. The peculiarities of sound are most noticeable in public speaking. Sometimes it seems to me that I am screaming; then again the sound is very low. In company, to carry on a conversation is very embarrassing. It affects my nervous system so much that I am unable to remain in the room. My deafness debars me from occupying positions of trust, and on several occasions I have been rejected or defeated on account of my deafness. I am unable even to hold positions in my own church, and all on account of my disability."

## EXHIBIT 19.

J. W. E. AGE 58. BUCHANAN, KENTUCKY.
8TH WEST VIRGINIA INFANTRY AND 7TH WEST VIRGINIA CAVALRY.

APPROXIMATING TOTAL DEAFNESS IN BOTH EARS.
CAUSED BY SUNSTROKE AND DISEASE IN HEAD.

"Was a teacher by profession until 1876, when I was compelled to give this up and take anything I could find to earn a living. I have been unable to do any manual labor for three years. I have distressing noises in my ears, from the hissing of steam to distant thunder. There is no let up day or night."

## EXHIBIT 20.

W. F. S. AGE 52. CHOPTAUK, MARYLAND.
12TH MASSACHUSETTS INFANTRY AND UNITED STATES NAVY.

APPROXIMATING TOTAL DEAFNESS OF BOTH EARS.
CAUSED BY EXPLOSION OF SHELL, AND INCREASED FROM AN ATTACK OF FEVER WHILE ON THE U. S. S. TALLAPOOSA, AT GALVESTON, TEXAS.

"I was a mariner by occupation before my service in the navy, and served in all the grades, from a boy up, in ship trading to California, China, the Indies and Europe. I had good reason to believe that I had a fair chance of success in my occupation. My experience and capacity would have insured me constant and profitable employment, but on account of my disability I was forced to quit the sea for a living.

"I suffer very much from vertigo, causing nausea and sometimes vomiting; also, noise in my head, which is a perpetual whirr of disagreeable sounds, occasional snapping, like explosions; also, loss of memory and bad health. I have no trade. My deafness has completely ruined all my prospects in life. I have nothing to look to; no end in view. All expectations of success, pleasure or profit are gone. All ambition is useless."

## EXHIBIT 21.

J. S. Age 52. Helena, Montana.
36 Wisconsin.

—

Totally Deaf in Both Ears, and Loss of Voice.
Caused by Exposure and Concussion.

"I have been in Helena eighteen months, and have yet to find the man who will give me employment. I have to talk by signs. I have terrible pains at times in my eyes, ears and head. I also have dizziness, and stagger, especially after dark. I was in the mail service several years in Iowa, but lost my place because I could not hear. With the few boarders my wife has, and my pension money, we manage to make a living. I could do light work, but no one will stop long enough to talk with me, and say it is too much trouble to make me understand. I have no regrets, but think the Government has not done for the deaf what it has done for those who are maimed, and are better qualified to earn a living for oneself and family."

## EXHIBIT 22.

J. E. B. Age 52. Nunda, Illinois.
D. 95th Illinois Infantry.

Total Deafness in Both Ears.
Caused by Shell Wound on Head.

"Being a farmer by occupation, I sought to keep the wolf from the door by cultivating and improving my small farm; but from inability to hear I met with many disadvantages in disposing of my products, and met with so much loss I had to dispose of my farm, being unable to manage it myself for reason of my total disability to hear and do manual labor. I suffer very much with severe pains in my head, and have perpetual ringing and roaring noises in my ears. Am often so dizzy that I am unable to stand up, and have to lie down until the dizziness leaves me.

"Aside from the performance of manual labor, deafness adds a chapter unknown to all other disabilities, inasmuch as it totally destroys all our social relations and makes a man a hermit, even with his neighbors. I regard the loss of my social faculties as the crowning misfortune of my life. Could I but hear the sweet tones of wife and children—yes, and the warm greetings of my old and cherished comrades that marched and fought by my side—it would be an elysium second only to the Aspen Bowers of the New Jerusalem.

"What is there left for me to do in this world that I may support myself and family?"

## EXHIBIT 23.

O. S. C. Age 48. Pulaski, New York.
New York Heavy Artillery.

Total Deafness in Left Ear, and Severe in Right.
Caused by Ball Entering in Front of the Left Ear Just Below the Temple. Voice Also Injured.

"The roaring in my ears at times sounds like a train of cars running across a bridge, and my sight will fail me for a few minutes, everything turning dark. After this distressing feeling passes off it will leave me totally deaf for some time.

"I have formerly worked on a farm, but am unable to do any manual labor, and am deprived of the means of support because I am deaf."

## EXHIBIT 24.

G. W. Age 55. Waverly, New York.
United States Light Artillery.

Severely Deaf in Both Ears.
Caused by Explosion of a Limber Chest and Concussion of Artillery.

"I am by occupation a railroad bridge builder, but not being able to do manual labor, had to give up this kind of work for something lighter and less dangerous. The injury from explosion also affects my lower limbs so much that I can hardly walk. I am not able to do one-third of a day's work, and am growing less able every year. I have frequent attacks of dizziness which makes it unsafe for me to be around machinery."

## EXHIBIT 25.

J. H. Age 49. Johnsville, Maryland.
B, 7th Maryland Infantry.

Severely Deaf in Both Ears, Approximating Total.
Caused by Chills, Fever and Exposure.

"I am a carpenter and painter by trade, and follow the latter when able, but on account of my disability I can not earn a living from my trade. I have many disagreeable noises in my head, with pains over my eyes, followed by dizziness and blindness. Have had several accidents by being run over, and all on account of my deafness."

## EXHIBIT 26.

R. M. C. Age 59. Des Moines, Iowa.
United States Signal Corps.

---

Severe Deafness in Both Ears.
Caused by Sunstroke.

"I was a teacher when I enlisted, but when discharged, in 1865, I was unfit to resume my profession of teacher on account of my deafness. I found other work, but was always behind and at a disadvantage to myself and employer, until I had to give up all business. I could not hear the orders given me. The roaring noise in my head and ears never stops, and almost sets me crazy.

"I have made several applications for clerical work in the Government service, but was refused on account of my deafness. No one wants me; I am in the way. What I am to do I can not answer."

## EXHIBIT 27.

D. P. W. Age 49. Colo, Iowa.
C and I, 10th Missouri Volunteers. Served 3 Years.

---

Totally Deaf in Left Ear, and Severely in the Right.
Caused by Severe Cold, Chills and Exposure.

"I am tortured with incessant ringing in my ears, and am unable to locate the direction of sounds. After I returned from the Union Army I took up farming and school teaching, but was unable to teach but three months, owing to my imperfect hearing and inability to endure the mental strain of teaching. I have been almost disabled from farm labor for over ten years on account of brain trouble, nervous prostration, headache and inability to perform manual labor. I am unfit for any work that requires stooping over. My affliction seems to cause every one to shun me, even in my own family."

## EXHIBIT 28.

G. W. Age 45. Kingston, New York.
I, 120th New York Infantry.

Totally Deaf in Both Ears
Caused by Exposure While a Prisoner at Andersonville, Ga.

"Before entering the service I was a druggist. On my return home my deafness interfered with my following the drug business. I have tried many other kinds of employment, but have failed in all on account of my not being able to hear. I have no occupation at present, and find it impossible to get employment at anything because men do not want to be bothered with a deaf man; not even will our government give employment to the deaf, as my experience has demonstrated the fact "

## EXHIBIT 29.

T. H. Age 57. Moscow, Idaho Territory.
D, 7th Iowa Cavalry.

Totally Deaf in Left Ear and Nearly So in Right.
Caused by Catarrh, Induced by Sickness and Exposure.

"I am troubled with an unpleasant roaring in my ears, especially in my right ear, and dizziness which requires me to use a cane to steady me in walking. When I entered the service, I was both a teacher and preacher, teaching being my permanent occupation. When I was discharged, my deafness prevented me from teaching, but not enough to prevent me from discharging the duties of a preacher. So long as my right ear remained slightly deaf I got along quite well, receiving a good salary. As the deafness increased my appointments became less remunerative, until several years ago I was compelled, only on account of difficulty of hearing, to give up my profession, and am now entirely deprived of salary. Having no employment left me in my old age, my case is a very hard one. There is no money consideration that would remunerate me for the loss of hearing."

## EXHIBIT 30.

B. S. Age 50. Berlin, Wisconsin.
B, 49th Wisconsin Infantry.

Totally Deaf in One Ear and Severely in the Other.
Caused by Catarrh.

"I am a farmer by occupation, and to tell you how my deafness interferes and troubles me in my business, is more than I can do."

## EXHIBIT 31.

D. M. Age 47. Knightstown, Indiana.
Indiana Volunteers.

Severely Deaf in Both Ears.
Caused by Concussion of Artillery and Exposure.

"My occupation is a wagon and carriage-maker. I am unable to get much work, and most of that through the assistance of sympathetic friends. People do not want to take the time or bother in talking to me; and another has to do the talking for me, and make the contract often at such low figures that I am not able to make one-fourth of what I could make if not deaf."

## EXHIBIT 32.

R. J. S. Age 47. Brookville, Indiana.
K, 101st Indiana Infantry.

Totally Deaf in Left Ear and Nearly So in Right.
Caused by Typhoid Fever and Catarrh.

"Am troubled with dizziness and imaginary sounds. I am totally disabled from performing manual labor in my former occupation as farmer or teacher."

## EXHIBIT 33.

W. B. Age 45. Stromsburg, Nebraska.
74th Indiana Infantry.

Approximating Total Deafness of Both Ears.
Caused From a Severe Wound in Right Ear.

"I am very much distressed with noises in my ears and dizziness with severe pains. I am also disabled in my feet, and am unable to perform manual labor of any kind, consequently have no occupation or employment."

## EXHIBIT 34

W. W. W. Age 47. Rome, New York.
D, 10th New York Cavalry.

Totally Deaf in Both Ears.
Caused From Exposure and Sickness.

"I have no trade or regular occupation. When I could hear railroading was my vocation, and while conductor I received $85 per month. Have been steward in a hotel, but as my deafness increased was obliged to relinquish such positions. I tried gardening and running a lawn mower; would be sent on errands. I was anxious to please, and rather than put them to the trouble of writing, I would get part of the order and guess at the rest. When I made a mistake it cut me to the heart to see the sneer and curl of the lip. The result was my discharge. Now that I am totally deaf there is nothing for me to do.

"In our city is a comrade who has been elected constable; is endorsed by all parties; receives the cream of the business; people cross the street to extend their sympathy and shake his hand. I come along behind him. I served three times as long as he did. I lost my hearing in both ears; he lost his arm. The same people who crossed the street to shake his hand will cross back to avoid speaking to me because they might be obliged to write a few words, and consider me a nuisance.

"While I am unable to hear any sound whatever, I am never free from distressing noises in my ears both day and night. I am unable to walk properly, and do not step with the same confidence of one who can hear. A maimed comrade has a hundred opportunities of earning a living where a totally deaf man has one. I would gladly exchange both of my legs for the restoration of my hearing. I begged the other day for a situation as tobacco stripper in a cigar factory, and could not get it because I was deaf. I am so crippled in my back that I can not perform manual labor? Hoping God and a merciful Congress will hear our prayers for an equitable rating for total and severe cases of deafness."

## EXHIBIT 35.

A. C. Age 50. Waverly, New York
U. S. Engineers (Artificer).

Deafness in Both Ears.
Caused by Heavy Artillery Firing.

"My deafness is a great impediment to my earning a living and working at my trade (carpenter), which causes me to work on roofs and scaffolding, and on account of dizziness I am unable to take the risks, and am at a disadvantage in procuring remunerative employment. Can not locate a sound without seeing from what direction it comes."

## EXHIBIT 36.

S. E. J. Age 51. Indianapolis, Indiana.
2d Indiana Battery.

Totally Deaf in Right Ear and Severely in Left.
Caused by Exposure.

"Have imaginary sounds in my left ear, like the escaping of steam or a hissing noise.

"When I entered the service I was a book-binder. I have always been foreman in the shops where I worked, and received the best of wages; but now I have to work at the bench at low wages because I can not hear well enough to transact business satisfactorily with my employers."

## EXHIBIT 37.

R. C. B. Aged 60. North Hyde Park, Vermont.
G, 3d Vermont.

Totally Deaf in Right Ear and Severely in the Left.
Caused by Sunstroke.

"My occupation before entering the army was teaching in winter and laying brick and plastering in summer. My deafness deprives me of teaching, and vertigo (from sunstroke) almost totally disables me for manual labor. I am now trying to work on a farm, and there are only a very few things I can do there on account of stooping and reaching up.

"The worst of all is the everlasting ringing noise in my head. Sometimes it is as water dropping, ringing of steel plate, roaring of waterfall, striking an anvil, etc.

"I used to earn three dollars a day; now I can not earn seventy-five cents, and have to board myself."

## EXHIBIT 38.

A. T. M. Age 57. Kenton, Ohio.
C, 82d Ohio Infantry.

Totally Deaf in Left Ear and Nearly So in the Right.
Caused by Exposure and Catarrh.

"I am a tailor by trade, and can work only under great difficulty, and then only occasionally, on account of vertigo and dizziness."

## EXHIBIT 39.

B. W. AGE 65. MARINE, ILLINOIS.
K, 43D ILLINOIS VOLUNTEERS.

TOTALLY DEAF IN LEFT EAR AND SEVERELY IN RIGHT.
CAUSED BY BILLIOUS FEVER. ALSO HAVE RHEUMATISM RESULTING IN HEART DISEASE.

"I am a plasterer by trade, but unable to perform any manual labor."

## EXHIBIT 40.

L. F. AGE 49. WAPOKENETA, OHIO.
1ST OHIO LIGHT ARTILLERY.

TOTALLY DEAF IN ONE EAR AND VERY SEVERE DEAFNESS OF THE OTHER.
CAUSED BY A HORSE STEPPING ON MY HEAD, RESULTING IN AN INTERNAL SORE.

"I have severe pains in my head nearly all the time. I am incapacitated from all kinds of labor, except a very little light work."

## EXHIBIT 41.

G. K. AGE 54. RUPTON, VERMONT.
K, 7TH VERMONT VOLUNTEERS.

TOTALLY DEAF IN BOTH EARS.
CAUSED BY EXPOSURE.

"I have no trade or occupation. Worked on a farm when I could get anything to do, but I am now unable to find work of any kind. People do not want to bother with me, and I have nothing but my pension I am as poor as poor can be."

## EXHIBIT 42.

A. J. A. AGE 44. NORTH TOPEKA, KANSAS.
CAPTAIN 2D INDIANA CAVALRY.

TOTAL DEAFNESS OF LEFT EAR AND SEVERE OF RIGHT.
CAUSED BY EXPOSURE AND BAD TREATMENT WHILE A PRISONER IN ANDERSONVILLE PRISON, GA.

"My deafness is variable in right ear, and at times nearly total. I am constantly annoyed with distressing sounds in my ears like the noise of millions of locusts. I am a druggist by profession, and can truly say if I were in the employ of any one I could not earn my salt. My deafness totally disqualifies me for a salesman. I also have heart difficulty, the result of rheumatism."

## EXHIBIT 43.

J. K. Age 51. Fountain City, Wisconsin.
Private 6th Wisconsin Infantry, and K, 22d V. R. C.

Totally Deaf in Left Ear and Severe in Right.
Caused by Severe Shell Wound.

"Have continuous pains in my head, with frequent dizziness and ringing noises, which is growing worse with advancing age. I also suffer from scurvy, which disease still clings to me, and especially in my legs My occupation was farming, before and after my enlistment, but am now able to do little or no manual labor."

## EXHIBIT 44.

C. A. O. Age 56. Edgerton, Minnesota.
Private K, 5th Iowa Cavalry.

Severe Deafness of Both Ears.
Caused by Concussion From Artillery.

"Have been a farmer for several years, but am unable to do manual labor. Have other disabilities, contracted while in the service. My deafness distresses me greatly from the perpetual roaring and snapping sounds in my ears, and dizziness. By reason of my severe deafness I am prevented from securing a more lucrative position in either the professions or mercantile pursuits, and my inability to hear has frequently subjected me to pecuniary losses."

## EXHIBIT 45.

B. A. C. Age 45. Lincoln, Nebraska
Volunteer Service.

Severely Deaf in Both Ears, Approximating Total.
Caused by Exposure, Etc.

"I would give everything I possess on this earth if I could have my hearing restored. It is the curse of my life. My deafness is growing worse every day, and nothing can help me."

## EXHIBIT 46.

G. L. Age 43. Robinsonville, Pennsylvania.
Pennsylvania Volunteers

Total Deafness of One Ear and Severe in the Other.
Caused by Exposure, Etc.

"I have tried farming for a living, and blacksmithing, but had to relinquish all on account of my inability to perform manual labor and to hear."

## EXHIBIT 47.

J. C. Age 46. Morris, New York.
2d New York Heavy Artillery.

Approximating Total Deafness of Both Ears.
Caused by Shell Wound

"I am a farmer by occupation, but owing to my deafness no one wants me. I have such distressing noise in my head like the ringing of bells, blowing of steam whistles and other sounds that make me nearly crazy. I am very dizzy all the time and unable to do manual labor."

## EXHIBIT 48.

A. W. Age 53. St Joseph, Missouri.
13th and 25th Missouri Infantry

Severe Deafness of Both Ears, Which, at Periods, is Total.
Caused by Exposure, Etc.

"I suffer very much from rheumatism, nervous prostration, terrible rumbling noises in my ears, severe pains in my head, caused by the perforation of both ear drums. The disability impairs my mind very much, which alone would keep me from my occupation, that of a blacksmith. I have tried many kinds of work, but have had to give them all up on account of my deafness and not being able to perform manual labor.

## EXHIBIT 49.

J. A. P. Age 47. Jamestown, New York.
A, 112th New York Infantry.

Totally Deaf in One Ear, and Nearly So in the Other.
Deafness Caused by Exposure.

"I have dizziness, and pains over my eyes, nervousness, and ringing noises in my ears like millions of grasshoppers in the room. I am a carpenter and joiner by trade, but can not get work half of the time, as the bosses do not want to bother with me on account of not hearing their orders."

## EXHIBIT 50.

P. McI. Age 42. Orange, Massachusetts.
Served in the 19th Corps.

Severely Deaf in Both Ears.
Caused by Exposure and Concussion of Artillery.

"Have noises in my ears like the singing of crickets. Am a machinist by trade, but owing to my imperfect hearing my occupation becomes unsafe and of no use to me. I can only get odd jobs to do now, and at small wages."

## EXHIBIT 51.

C. F. P. Age 63. Winona, Minnesota.
E, 16th Wisconsin Infantry.

Totally Deaf in Right Ear, and Approximating Total in Left.
Caused by Exposure and Catarrh.

"My trade is a blacksmith, but owing to my deafness and nervous debility I am unable to work at my trade. I am troubled continually with distressing noises in my ears I am troubled also with dizziness, and so badly at times that I have to take hold of something to keep from falling. I have no occupation at the present time, and find it impossible to get any work. No one wants me around; I am considered in the way and in danger of being hurt. I have a trumpet and dentiphone, but receive little or no benefit from them.

## EXHIBIT 52.

C. L. Age 45. Lunenburg, Massachusetts.
D, 7th Rhode Island Volunteers.

Total Deafness in Left Ear, and Severe in Right.
Caused by Concussion From a Bursting Shell.

"I am suffering very much from dizziness, rush of blood to the head, and nervousness. By occupation a carpenter, which I had to relinquish on account of the liability from accident. Am out of employment eight to ten months in the year, and all on account of my deafness. I am totally unable to perform manual labor, and am at present on a farm with a comrade to keep from going to the poor-house."

## EXHIBIT 53.

M. E. S. Age 44. St. Louis, Missouri.
F, 43d O. V. I. and B, 88th O. V. I.

Severe Deafness in Both Ears, Approximating Total.
Caused From Exposure and Catarrh.

"My occupation is a carpenter, but owing to my increased deafness I have tried other work, and have failed signally, until I am perplexed to find out what there is to do in this world for a deaf man. I have been discharged from so many positions, and for no other reason than my disability, that I have become discouraged. I have all the unpleasant noises in my ears and other peculiarities that the deaf are never free from.

## EXHIBIT 54.

H. G. Age 55. Poughkeepsie, New York.
United States Navy.

Nearly Total Deafness of Both Ears.
Caused by Shell Wound Splitting Left Temple and Injuring Left Hip and Right Leg.

"Am subject to dizziness to such a degree that I often have to hold on to objects to support myself. I find it almost impossible to secure employment. No one wants me because I can not hear. I have not earned $20 in three months, and no prospect for me in the future."

## EXHIBIT 55.

L. H. G. Age 55. Benton, Kansas.
3d Indiana Cavalry.

Total Deafness of One Ear and Nearly so of the Other.
Caused by Measles and Severe Cold.

"Have all the conglomeration of disagreeable noises inherited by the deaf. I am by trade a blacksmith, but am unable to do manual labor. I can not get light work such as I am able to do. No one wants to hire me at any price, because I am deaf."

## EXHIBIT 56.

S. C. S. Age 58. Lena, Illinois.
Private, D, 7th Michigan Infantry.

Total Deafness of Left Ear and Severe of Right.
Caused from an Attack of Measles, Exposure and Catarrh, Resulting Also in Disease of the Lungs.

"Present and former occupation, physician. Can not hear sounds of heart or lungs, nor lectures, sermons, prattle of children, music, nor can I take part in conversation. I am unable to support myself by my profession, and can not engage in any other pursuits on account of my deafness. Owing to my lung trouble, am unable to perform manual labor. I frequently have distressing sounds like an explosion in my ears, followed by dizziness."

## EXHIBIT 57.

C. G. W. Age 50. Belvidere, Illinois.
95th Illinois Infantry.

Total Deafness of Right Ear and Severe of Left.
Caused by Exposure, Sickness and Concussion from Heavy Siege Guns at Vicksburg, Mississippi.

"Owing to other disabilities I can not perform manual labor. No one wants me because I can not hear their orders; and I must trust to my pension and the few light jobs I can get to make a living."

## EXHIBIT 58.

C. H. P. Age 47. Adrian, Michigan.
K, 14th Michigan Infantry.

Totally Deaf in Right Ear and Severely in Left.
Caused by Exposure and Cold at the Battle of Stone River.

"I worked formerly at my trade, carpenter, at two dollars a day, but on account of piles and deafness am unable to do manual labor. I work when I can get anything to do at odd jobs that will enable me to support myself and family I have not earned to exceed fifty dollars a year for the last five years.

"I have continual distressing noises in my ears, and at times a cracking sound followed by dizziness that will disable me for several hours at a time.

"The suffering from inflammation and pains in my ears often confines me to my room for weeks."

## EXHIBIT 59.

J. M. H. Age 43. Plymouth, Indiana.
K, 13th Indiana Cavalry.

Totally Deaf in Both Ears.
Caused by Concussion of Heavy Artillery, Bursting Both Ear Drums.

"I am a farmer by occupation, and am only able to do light chores. I am a farmer by compulsion, as I am unable to find or secure any other kind of employment. For the past twenty-three years I have scarcely had one undisturbed night's rest. Every night when I lie down to rest, the conglomeration of imaginary noises begin, dogs howling, children crying, men quarreling, cannon booming. I can not sleep, and only find relief by getting up and take my needed rest in an old arm chair, until the early dawn awakens me, and I get up without feeling the refreshing rest that I so much crave. I have a tired feeling, unfitting me for the duties even of a farm.

"Is there no help, no relief for our great affliction?"

## EXHIBIT 60.

R. M. Age 67. Marble, Arkansas.
Late Corporal Co. A, West Virginia Cavalry.

Totally Deaf in Right Ear, and Nearly so in Left.
Caused by Gun-shot Wound, Shattering Jaw-bone and Knocking Out My Teeth, Passing Back Into My Head.

"I am totally disabled from earning my living, and am also troubled with dizziness, neuralgia, pains in my head, with impairment of sight—the result of my wounds."

## EXHIBIT 61.

J. R. J. Age 45. Plainfield, Indiana.
A, 70th Indiana Infantry.

Severe Deafness of Both Ears, Approximating Total.
Caused by Concussion of Shell at Battle of New Hope Church, Georgia.

"I suffer very much from nervous prostration and general debility. Am unable to get employment at my trade, painter, or even other light work, as people do not want to be bothered with a deaf man. I also have other disabilities, which cause intense pains through the head, neck and breast, which disables me from performing manual labor. I also have much dizziness and vertigo, which is another bar to earning a living."

## EXHIBIT 62.

J. W. H. Age 48. Syracuse, New York.
Battery C, New York Artillery.

Total Deafness of Both Ears.
Caused by Explosion of Shell and Concussion.

"Have not been able for years to work at my former trade, carpenter and bridge builder. For the past few years I have not been able to get any employment, even light office work. I have tried to get work in the Postoffice Department, and in the new Government Building. They say, 'What can you do? You are deaf; we can't use you.' So it goes, everywhere. I am terribly annoyed with ringing and buzzing noises in my ears that confuses me to think what I am doing. To stoop over causes dizziness. I am in constant danger in getting around after night. Broken down in health, unable to perform manual labor, or find any kind of light employment. I am discouraged; for the future looks dark and dismal for me in my total disability as far as earning a living for ones self and family."

## EXHIBIT 63.

J. S. Age 50. Lebanon, Pennsylvania.
17th Pennsylvania Cavalry.

Totally Deaf, and Blind in Left Eye.
Caused by Fever and Ague, Exposure and Too Much Quinine.

"My occupation before enlisting was a laborer, but since 1875 I have not been able to perform any manual labor, being without education and unable to secure any employment, and must depend on my pension for bread. I have all kinds of noises in my head, with dizziness, which increases as I grow older."

## EXHIBIT 64.

G. C. Age 54. Wamego, Kansas.
24th Indiana Battery.

Totally Deaf of Left Ear, and Nearly So of the Right.
Caused by Concussion of Artillery During the Siege of Knoxville, Tenn.

"By occupation a laborer, but not being able to perform manual labor, I am thankful for anything that will enable me to make a living. My disability grows worse with each year. I find it almost impossible to secure employment of any kind. The public do not want to hire me on account of my deafness."

## EXHIBIT 65.

J. B. W. Age 48. Muscatine, Iowa.
35th Iowa Infantry.

Variable Deafness of Both Ears, in Damp Weather Approximating Total.
Caused From Exposure and Sickness, Resulting in Perforation of Both Ear Drums.

"Also have disease of the heart, and, with my deafness, am incapable of performing manual labor of any kind. Have not been able to do any work for four years. Former occupation, janitor of a church."

## EXHIBIT 66.

J. F. Q. Age 51. Le Sueur Center, Minnesota.
Battery C, 1st Illinois Light Artillery.

Totally Deaf in Right and Nearly So in Left Ear.
Caused by Accident During the Battle of Atlanta, Georgia, from a Tree Falling on Me, Resulting in Injury to My Head, and Catarrh.

"By occupation a school teacher, but unable to earn a living from this vocation. By the assistance of my wife, who hears for me, I have been able to keep from going to the poor-house by doing little jobs of writing; but do not think it will last long enough to provide the means to support myself and family."

## EXHIBIT 67.

P. K. Age 47. Suspension Bridge, New York.
B, 151st New York Volunteers.

Nearly Total Deafness of Both Ears.
Caused by Measles and Exposure.

"I was a farmer previous to my enlistment; am unable to do hard work of any kind, and can not stoop over without experiencing dizziness. I have a perpetual roaring and singing in my ears, more noise than a steam engine would make. It is simply impossible for me to secure employment other than farming, and I have to hire much of this done that I could do if I could hear."

## EXHIBIT 68.

F. H. Age 45. St. Joseph, Missouri.
1st Regiment Nebraska Infantry.

Severe Deafness of Both Ears.
Caused by Sickness and Concussion of Artillery.

"Have distressing noises in my ears, with dizziness, all the time. By occupation a laborer, in which my disability deters me from securing employment I could otherwise perform."

## EXHIBIT 69.

J. L. E. Age 54. Rohnerville, California.
G, 7th Illinois Infantry.

Approximating Total Deafness of Both Ears.
Caused by Severe Exposure at the Siege of Fort Donaldson, Resulting in Catarrh and Throat Complications.

"I enlisted in 1861, while a young physician, having a perfect hearing until the severe exposure, when my deafness soon after unfitted me for duty and I was discharged. My deafness increased so rapidly that in 1874 I was compelled to totally abandon my profession, and practically shuts me out from all remunerative employment which I am otherwise capable of performing.

"Besides the single fact of deafness, there are, in my case, many distressing noises. Among others, a continual roaring sound, like a body of falling water, accompanied at times with dizziness so great as to compel me to grasp the nearest object for support. My deafness is a greater loss to me than the loss of limbs, for with the latter disability I could still practice my profession, teach, operate a telegraph, take an agency, clerkship, or follow almost any business which deafness practically excludes me from.

"A year ago I was run down by a horse and cart; collar bone and two ribs broken, shoulder knocked out of place, nearly killed, and all this happened because I could not hear."

## EXHIBIT 70.

H. F. H. Age 47. Gilbert's Mills, New York.
A, 24th, and K, 184th New York Infantry.

Totally Deaf in One Ear and Nearly so in the Other.
Caused from Exposure and a Severe Cold.

"By occupation a contractor and mason from which I was earning $75 and $100 per month, but for the past three years I have been compelled to give up working at my trade, being wholly unfit to do manual labor on account of the stooping position and dizziness.

"I have the most strange noises in my head, at times like the clatter and noise of a planing mill. Every time I catch the least cold in my head I have snapping and sounds like the report of a gun, sometimes three or four in succession. My disability causes me to make many mistakes because I do not hear distinctly. For this reason I am unable to find or secure remunerative employment."

## EXHIBIT 71.

---

E. L. S. Age 56. Acworth, New Hampshire.
4th New Hampshire Infantry.

Severely Deaf in Both Ears.
Caused by Sickness After Parole from Exposure While Confined in Prison. Also Have Hernia on Right Side.

"I have a full calendar of distress—noises in my ears, such as the escaping of steam, music of organs, roaring of water and a thousand and one other sounds which would be impossible to make one believe who can hear. In my present condition I am unfit for nearly all kinds of business. Being subject to asthma deprives me from performing manual labor. I served my country nearly four years and six months. By occupation a farmer."

## EXHIBIT 72.

J. G. B. Age 47. St. Marys, Kansas.
Infantry.

Totally Deaf in One Ear, and Severely So in the Other.
Caused by Accident From Limb Falling on My Head in Making a Charge at Hines Bluff, in Rear of Vicksburg, Miss.

"No one can conceive what I have suffered from the distressing roaring and buzzing noises in my ears; frequently like an explosion so severe that I become unconscious. My distress and anxiety how to provide for myself and family give me more trouble than all else. I am unable to follow any occupation, as my memory is failing me, and when I want to collect my ideas together my head goes around in a circle. I suffer greatly with nervous prostration that nearly uses me up. I am totally incapacitated to follow any mechanical or business vocation. I enlisted in 1861 and mustered out in 1866."

## EXHIBIT 73.

R. C. H. Age 50. Assumption, Illinois.
32d Illinois Infantry.

Severely Deaf of Both Ears.
Caused by Explosion of Shell Near My Head at the Siege of Vicksburg, Miss.

"I entered the army with hearing unimpaired. I was fitted by education and training for business or professional career. Have had some experience in newspaper work, but by reason of my increasing deafness I have been obliged to give it up, as well as other business or professional pursuits. Am unable to get employment of any kind. I live on a farm, but can not do a day's work on account of rheumatism contracted while in the service. A neighbor and comrade of mine lost an arm in the service. He has acquired a competency in business. I should be rejoiced to exchange places with him, allowing him, of course, to keep his wealth. I have all kinds of roaring and other indescribable noises in my ears that almost set me wild."

## EXHIBIT 74

H. H. S. Age 54. Canonsburg, Pennsylvania.
D, 10th Pennsylvania Infantry.

Severely Deaf in Both Ears, Each Approaching Total.
Caused by a Wound in the Head in the Battle of the Wilderness.

"By occupation a shoemaker, and while I am not entirely prevented from working at my trade, however, from the fact of not being able to hear distinctly the orders of my customers or employers, I am liable to make errors, and makes me reluctant in taking orders. For this reason I have given up my trade, and now work at any kind of light labor that I can obtain, and where I deem it safe. In other words, I can not work where I can not *see* the danger, as I have nearly lost my life on two occasions by not being able to see the danger. My disability is gradually growing worse each year, and my voice is failing me."

## EXHIBIT 75.

J. L. P. Age 59. Mount Vernon, Wisconsin.
Captain 96th Illinois Infantry.

Severe Deafness of Both Ears, Gradually Approaching Total.
Caused by Exposure Near Dalton, Georgia, Bivouacing Without Shelter for Nearly Two Weeks; Also, Resulting in Rheumatism, Which Has Become Troublesome of Late Years.

"I am unable to perform manual labor. On my return from the service in 1865 I resumed the practice of medicine and drug business, my former occupation, but on account of my increased deafness I sold out in 1867 and took up farming, for which I was entirely unfitted by experience or otherwise, resulting in the loss of all my savings, and because of my inability to hear. What am I to do? I must have bread for my family. I can not earn it by manual labor; I can not sell goods over the counter, neither can I practice medicine. Not only are all the avenues of business closed to us, but all social intercourse with our families, to say nothing of the strain on our nervous system from the incessant noises in the ears. After I have laid awake all night, unable to sleep from this conglomeration of imaginary sounds, and it seemed that I should become distracted."

## EXHIBIT 76.

L. H. Age 53. North Branch, New York.
56th New York Volunteers.

Nearly Total Deafness of Both Ears.
Caused by Exposure and Catarrh.

"My occupation was a butcher, but on account of my deafness I am unable to support myself and family by my trade, nor even by farming, my present occupation. When I catch a little cold I become dizzy, my ears ache, and the noise in my head sounds like an engine. Before entering the service I made a good living by my trade, and now I have no resource left me to earn a living. What am I to do?"

## EXHIBIT 77.

H. G. Age 49. Wheeling, West Virginia.
114th Ohio Volunteers.

Total Deafness of the Right Ear and Severe of the Left.
Caused by Catarrh and Exposure.

"Was in business a few years after my return from the army, but had to give it up on account of the inconvenience of hearing. I am now working in a tobacco factory, doing the best I can. My disability has caused me indescribable suffering in vertigo, and several times have nearly fallen down. My ears are badly affected; have severe pains in my head nearly all the time; also, snapping noises in my ears like the striking of an anvil, sounds like the music from a hand-organ, then like thundering, and choking sensation while asleep. I would willingly exchange an arm or a leg, or even both, for the restoration of my health and hearing."

## EXHIBIT 78.

T. W. S. Age 55. Philadelphia, Pa.
D, 150th Indiana Infantry.

Approximating Total Deafness of Both Ears.
Caused by Exposure and Catarrh.

"I am by trade a shoemaker, and while, physically speaking, I may be able to pull a waxed thread as firmly as needed, but in the field of competition my affliction tells. If I seek employment from others I find they invariably prefer a man who can hear. I have a small repair shop, and find it necessary that my wife be near by to hear for me. I am like a tethered ox, confined to a certain area, without power to go beyond. I can say nothing about the social life of a deaf man. He has none.

"I am a constant sufferer with noises in my head of the most annoying and distressing nature; also dizziness and vertigo. I can give no estimate of the disadvantage I am at on account of my disability, because I can only see from the deaf side of the question. I am able to work, but the trouble is to get it.

"I feel pleased that the largest part of our earthly life is behind, and our suffering will soon be over."

## EXHIBIT 79.

G. E. A. Age 59. Fulton, New York.
110th New York Volunteers.

Approximating Total Deafness of Both Ears.
Caused by Exposure and Sickness, Resulting in Malarial Fever.

"By occupation a woolen manufacturer. When working at my trade I earned three dollars a day, but now I am unable to procure employment at any price, and all I have to support myself and family on is my pension. I am unfit to perform manual labor for reason of chronic diarrhea and rheumatism."

## EXHIBIT 80.

H. O. W. Age 48. Erie, Pennsylvania.
Twenty Years' Service in United States Marine Corps and Navy.

Total Deafness of Left Ear and Severe of Right.
Caused from Catarrhal Inflammation of Right and Left Middle Ear, from the Battle of Port Royal, South Carolina.

"Am easily affected by colds, which increase the whizzing noises in my ears. Can find no stable employment outside of my church janitorship because of the annoyance to those who would employ me. Am willing and anxious to work at light employment, as I am not physically strong enough to do manual labor. Never had a trade, consequently have no chance in this avenue. Power of apprehension very dull. Use no artificial means to make myself hear."

## EXHIBIT 81.

R. T. Age 77. National Military Home, Kansas.
37th Iowa Infantry.

Total Deafness of Both Ears.
Caused by Severe Cold and Exposure.

"Have no occupation; have been unable to do manual labor for 15 years past on account of deafness and rheumatism. Have to use canes to support myself in getting around."

## EXHIBIT 82.

W. H. B. Age 51. Burlington, Kansas.
B, 11th Missouri Cavalry.

Approximating Total Deafness of Both Ears.
Caused from Long Exposure on the March and Bivouac.

"On account of chronic diarrhea and deafness my nervous system is so weakened and shattered that at times I can not write a legible hand. After my return from the army I taught penmanship for awhile, and then I have done some clerical work in the public offices, but as my deafness continues to grow worse and being so nervous at times that my occupation is about gone. Being so deaf as not to hear ordinary conversation, I can not get employment where I might if not deaf."

## EXHIBIT 83.

L. T. Age 55 Des Moines, Iowa.
G, 35th Wisconsin Infantry.

Nearly Totally Deaf in Both Ears.
Caused by an Explosion of a Shell in Spanish Fort, Mobile Harbor.

"I am a printer by occupation and still follow my trade when I can secure work. For the last twenty years it has been very difficult for me to secure employment, from the fact that proprietors of printing establishments will not employ deaf men if they can get others. I am a first-class workman and strictly temperate. Some years I have not been able to secure ten weeks' work in each year, and then I get it because there is no good printer who will accept it. I have made application to both State and Federal government for some position, but my petition was rejected on the ground that 'Your deafness will bar you from filling any position.' Next to the blind, those who have lost their hearing are the worst handicapped in making a living; and I think it had been better had we met the fate of those who fell in battle than to live our silent life and endure the unequal contest for the necessaries of life."

## EXHIBIT 84.

J. P. H. Age 59. Franklin Iron Works, New York.
B, 189th New York Volunteers.

Total Deafness of Right Ear and Severe of Left.
Caused by Cold and Exposure Resulting in Chronic Catarrh While Bivouacing at Appomattox C. H., Virginia.

"From prostrations aggravated by general debility of my whole system, I am unable to converse with my own children or carry on a conversation with anyone. I have a perpetual noise in my head, roaring, buzzing, hissing sounds, and at times sounds like there was thousands of imps talking and quarreling, almost driving me wild. I was employed as baggagemaster on a railroad until 1869, when I was discharged on account of my increased deafness. I received in wages and scale money about $75 per month, and after I lost my position on the railroad I could get no work except an occasional charity job, until a few years ago I got a position getting out coal and coke dust at a blast furnace at the munificent salary of $20 per month, while my companions in the railroad's employ are holding honorable and remunerative positions, and I am left out as good for nothing because I am deaf."

## EXHIBIT 85.

H. F. Age 60. Erie, Pennsylvania.
United States Navy for 13 Years.

Total Deafness of Both Ears.
Caused by a Blow from the Rear Lever of a 10-Inch Gun on Board of the U. S. Steamer Dakota.

"I am troubled constantly with peculiar and distressing noises in my ears like the escaping of steam and buzzing of millions of bees. I also have throat trouble and nervousness that troubles me in my sleep My former occupation was a mariner. Am unable to obtain employment of any kind, and have not done any work for three years."

## EXHIBIT 86.

C. O. H. Age 50. Warren, Ohio.
Ohio Volunteers.

Totally Deaf in Left Ear, and Nearly So in Right.
Caused by Exposure, Producing Catarrh.

"I suffer the most distressing and various noises in both ears, sometimes for days; such a racket that it nearly makes me wild, leaving me nervous and irritable. I was formerly engaged in mercantile business, and no doubt would have been more successful had it not been for my infirmity, and nearly four years ago was compelled to give up my business on account of my increasing disability. Since that time I have not been engaged in any occupation, neither do I see any branch of business open for me in my great calamity. Had I lost an arm or leg, or even both legs, I can see many avenues opened where I could make a living and be useful and successful, beside the enjoyment of social and intellectual life: and, above all, hearing the voices of my family. I was about to make application for a position in some of the departments at Washington, but I find I am disqualified on account of my deafness. If our Government will not give me employment because I am deaf, who will?"

## EXHIBIT 87.

J. H. J. Age 54. Roaring Springs, Pennsylvania.
C, 192d Pennsylvania Volunteers.

Nearly Totally Deaf in Both Ears.
Caused From Injury and Disease Resulting in Catarrh.

"My case is a severe one, having an invalid wife, with no gainful employment for me to meet the wants of the sick, or to procure the comforts and necessaries of life to allay their sufferings. I am nearly as helpless as if blind. I am afraid our law-makers at Washington do not realize the great disadvantage a totally or severely deaf man is placed in, competing with those who can hear, and overlook the fact that we are a totally disabled class when it comes to earning a living for one's self and family.

"We are even barred from doing what we know how to do, because we are not able to fulfill our part at the proper time, owing to our deafness. In the presence of a passing humanity, we are as one born deaf and dumb; can not hear when spoken to, and do not receive the intonation of the human voice, and apparently dumb, because we do not speak. Hence, we are void of any ability to earn a support. The employer of this day and generation looks for the hearing ear, as well as for the free and willing heart. Our hearts grow weak, owing to our many failures, with a full share of all the calamities, with little or none of the pleasures and enjoyments of society; we are doomed to live the life of the living, but dead to the world and our friends."

## EXHIBIT 88.

J. J. R. Age 45. Hamburg, Iowa.
2d Iowa Infantry

Approximating Total Deafness of Both Ears.
Caused From Accident During the Battle of Shiloh.

"A cannon-shot struck my gun barrel, which was on my shoulder, driving it against my head, knocking me down, causing blood to flow from my nose and ears, and my eyes to become bloodshot, when I found I was partially unconscious, and any effort I made to walk would be in a circle. The accident caused concussion of the brain, resulting as above stated. By occupation I am a harness maker, but owing to the jar in pulling the wax ends I am unable to work at my trade. Since I have been compelled to quit work I feel like a criminal chained to a skeleton, life linked to death, as it were, in despair. Who can imagine or describe the misery caused by the loss of hearing? What unnumbered sources of enjoyment are closed to the deaf? They are sufferers through life, objects of pity and compassion, constantly in danger, condemned to a solitary existence, all the more terrible from the life and animation around them, seen but unheard. How many deaf soldiers, with all necessary business qualifications to insure success, are forced to a life of dependence on charity through the misfortune? So many are in poverty and distress because of the loss of this most necessary of the senses.

"I am never free from the horrible noises in my ears and dizziness in walking, especially after dark. When stooping over I become blind, with imaginary objects dancing in front of my eyes; have constant roaring and rumbling sounds in my head, noises like distant thunder, artillery, blowing off steam, noise heard in a planing mill, and a very disagreeable sound like some old person talking in an adjacent room with a cracked voice. This noise is the most distressing, and leaves me unfit for all kinds of business. How often have we seen the smirking smile at our expense when trying to understand, they forgetting for the time that our misfortune is no crime. Though deaf, we are not dumb or blind."

## EXHIBIT 89.

C. W. B. Age 65. Dayton, Oregon.
14th Iowa Infantry.

Totally Deaf in Both Ears.
Caused From Exposure and Sickness, Resulting in Catarrh.

"I wish I had lost an arm or leg; I would enjoy the rest of my days better than being totally deaf. I have six children. I had to let four of them go to other homes, and have got two boys with me, and am too poor to keep them in boots and clothes; they need boots now the worst kind, and it makes me cry to look at my poor little fellows. They complain of pain, and it is caused by not having clothes to keep them warm. I am sick, too; sick four days out of every week. What a hell! I can not believe in a worse one, and it is because I am totally deaf and sick."

## EXHIBIT 90.

S. J. S. Age 44. Portsmouth, Ohio.
F, 140th Ohio Infantry.

Approximating Total Deafness of Both Ears.
Caused by Exposure from Sleeping on the Cold Ground While Wet, Without Shelter.

"I have all the distressing noises in my ears that the deaf are heir to. For the last eight years I have found employment at a fire-brick works, where I have no communication with the foreman for days at a time. I have sought many other kinds of employment, but was refused on account of my deafness. I have frequent attacks of dizziness in my head, and have lost much time on account of it. I am very nervous and irritable. Have no companionship but my family."

## EXHIBIT 91.

W. H. H. G. Age 45. Cadillac, Michigan.
A, 3d Michigan Infantry.

Totally Deaf in Both Ears.
Caused by Concussion of Artillery.

"I entered the service at the age of 18. Was brought up on a farm. On my return from the service I was unfit for performing manual labor by reason of dizziness when work required a stooping position. I learned book-keeping, and have followed that occupation when I could get anything to do; but in this enlightened age of telephones, it has been only by the favor of intimate friends that I have had occasional temporary positions. My disability prevents me from obtaining remunerative employment, and I find it almost impossible to secure work in competition with the maimed comrades who can hear. I am unable to engage in any kind of business for myself without being in the power and at the mercy of everyone around me who can hear. I have a general impairment of health and strength resulting from the strains of army service, which renders it impossible for me to engage in any manual labor without breaking down entirely."

## EXHIBIT 92.

J. G. Y. Age 49. St. Joseph, Missouri.
B, 16th Illinois Infantry.

Nearly Total Deafness of Both Ears
Caused by Heavy Artillery Firing and Exposure on the Mississippi Campaign.

"I become so dizzy at times that I am unable to stand up. I also have noises in my ears like the ringing of bells and blowing of whistles. I am by occupation a skilled laborer in car-shops here, but owing to my general disability I am working, when able, at light work at greatly reduced wages on account of my not being able to hear."

## EXHIBIT 93.

P. C. W. Age 56. Gordon, Ohio.
D, 58th Ohio Infantry.

Severe Deafness of Both Ears.
Caused from Exposure and Sickness, Resulting in Catarrh and Pneumonia, After the Siege of Fort Donaldson and on the March to Fort Henry.

"By the favor of friends I am a Justice of the Peace, and I labor under many disadvantages in attending to the duties of the office, and no doubt lose much business on account of my deaf condition, and my disability is growing worse every year, and I will soon have to retire from all kinds of business and employment."

## EXHIBIT 94.

J. M. C. Age 52. Greensboro, Indiana.
31st Indiana Infantry.

Severe Deafness of Both Ears.
Caused from Gun-Shot Wound in the Battle of Lookout Mountain.

"I have many peculiar imaginary noises in my ears. The human voice sounds like it was at a great distance. My occupation before enlistment was farming, but was unable to resume the duties on account of my physical condition, not being able to do hard work. I labor under the greatest difficulty in obtaining the lightest work, even when I can find it to do. I have to support my aged mother and my children with whatever the government sees fit to give me."

## EXHIBIT 95

H. C. H. Age 57. Martinsville, Illinois.
Captain, G, 123d Illinois Infantry.

Approximating Total Deafness of Both Ears.
Caused by Exposure, Catarrh and Concussion From Artillery.

"My case is hopeless. There can be no cure, no relief. The ear-drum being broken from concussion, can not be restored. After an expenditure of $500, with no relief, money all gone, and reduced to abject poverty, I applied for a pension, and got the munificent rating of $2 per month, and dating my disability from twenty years after it occurred. To the present date I have not drawn as much money as pension as I have expended in treatment and in instruments and appliances to assist me in hearing. I am now growing old. I have to employ a man at a salary of $400 a year, whose business is principally to hear for me. Not only this, but I am cut off from most of the enjoyments of life; in fact, often feel life a burden, and wish it would end. I can not enjoy company, and walk from my merry companions frequently to seek seclusion. Cut off from all the pleasures of others in hearing, speaking, preaching, music, and even thunder, with close attention and hard scratching to make a living for my family, life truly is a burden."

## EXHIBIT 96

M. L. Age 46. Lansing, Michigan.
K, 7th Michigan Infantry.

Total Deafness of Both Ears, and Loss of Right Leg Above the Knee.
Caused From Wounds and Exposure at Battle of Gettysburg, Pa.

"I have been afflicted for twenty-six years with total deafness of both ears, coupled with loss of my right leg above the knee. If I could have my choice I would gladly exchange both my legs, or both my arms, if I could recover the valuable endowment, hearing, of both ears. Total deafness alone is a total disability, and should be pensioned next to the loss of sight. I find the faculty of hearing of much more importance than any other of the senses, and not to be compared with the loss of a limb or limbs. The deaf are left in a state of melancholy and hopeless isolation, which is but faintly appreciated by those always blessed with good, sound hearing."

## EXHIBIT 97.

W. H. T. Age 48. Weedsport, New York.
Battery F, 3d New York Light Artillery.

Approximating Total of Both Ears.
Caused from Exposure and Catarrh.

"I have severe and distressing shocks in my head, extending to the back of the neck. My former occupation was a sailor. I am debarred from this on account of my deafness, and can not find work. No one wants me because I can not hear their orders and commands. Everyone seems to avoid me."

## EXHIBIT 98.

A. W. P. Age 66. Fairport, New York.
13th and 50th New York Infantry.

Totally Deaf in Both Ears.
Caused by Fatigue and Severe Exposure While in a Rebel Prison.

"I have terrible ringing sounds in my head, and dizziness so bad that it is impossible for me to walk steady after dark. My former occupation was carriage-maker, but was obliged to give it up ten years ago, and since then have had no employment. Owing to scurvy, contracted while in prison, I am unable to do manual labor or obtain employment on account of my deafness."

## EXHIBIT 99.

J. V. B. Age 53. Waverly, New York.
E, 23d New York Infantry.

Approximating Total Deafness of Both Ears.
Caused by Exposure and Concussion at the Battle of Fredericksburg, Va.

"I am almost totally deaf. I have to use an earphone, which enables me to hear very little. My head distresses me all the time. I have a roaring in my head continually, and when I try to listen or hear it makes me dizzy and my head aches. I feel all tired out. My occupation was a lumber merchant and farmer before I enlisted. Since my discharge from the U. S. service I have had to employ a man to do my business for me because I was deaf."

## EXHIBIT 100.

W. E. P. Age 49. Salinas, California.
Battery, M. 2d Pennsylvania Heavy Artillery.

Approximating Total Deafness.
Caused From Typhoid Fever and Exposure.

"I am also disabled with chronic rheumatism, and am unable to perform manual labor of any kind. I have a perpetual distressing buzzing, roaring noise in my ears that unfits me for nearly all employment. I have no occupation, and am unable to obtain even the simplest work. No one wants me around because I am deaf and in the way. I am dependent, in part, for my support to my father and relatives, for my pension is insufficient to supply my simple wants and comforts."

## EXHIBIT 101.

N. A. S. Age 46. Pine Village, Indiana.
G. 100th Indiana Infantry.

Approximating Total Deafness of Both Ears.
Caused From Explosion of Shell at Lovejoy Station, Georgia.

"It will be impossible for me to express or describe the distressing feeling and noises in my ears that I must endure, both day and night, without cessation. When the wind blows I must wear ear-mufflers, or my head has a thousand noises, and pains me so severely I can not sleep or hear anything. There is scarcely a day that I am able to do manual labor on account of rheumatism.

"My former occupation was foreman in public works, but as my deafness advanced I was unable to perform the duties assigned me, and had to resign my position, for no other reason than my deafness. Since then I have worked as a common laborer, and am not wanted even as a laborer, or anything else, where the sense of hearing must be in use. Is there anything a deaf man can do to earn an honest living?"

## EXHIBIT 102.

Wm N. F. Age 59. Chardon, Ohio.
3d New York Light Artillery.

Total Deafness of Both Ears.
Caused from Exposure and Concussion of Artillery.

"Outer membrane of both ears ruptured, which causes great pain, accompanied by distressing sounds in both ears.

"Partially paralyzed from disease contracted while in the service. Have been unable to perform any labor for five years. Wholly dependent on pension for support."

# SUMMARY

*Of the One Hundred and Two Cases.*

| | |
|---|---|
| Total deafness of both ears | 36 |
| Approximating total deafness | 66 |
| Total | 102 |

## TABLE 1.—Branch of Service.

| | | | |
|---|---|---|---|
| Infantry | 55 | Navy | 6 |
| Cavalry | 16 | U. S. Signal Service | 1 |
| Light artillery | 15 | U. S. Engineers | 1 |
| Heavy artillery | 8 | | |

## TABLE 2.—Occupations.

| | | | |
|---|---|---|---|
| Physicians | 4 | Farmers | 15 |
| Preachers | 3 | Mechanics | 34 |
| Teachers | 8 | Mariners | 2 |
| Lawyers | 2 | Printers | 1 |
| Druggists | 4 | Telegraph operators | 2 |
| Merchants | 5 | Railroaders | 3 |
| Clerks | 6 | Unclassified | 11 |
| Contractors | 2 | | |

| | |
|---|---|
| Able to perform manual labor | 16 |
| Unable to perform manual labor | 86 |
| Total | 102 |

| | |
|---|---|
| Number who have no gainful occupations | 73 |
| Number who have occasional employment | 26 |
| Number who have steady employment | 3 |
| Total | 102 |

## TABLE 3.—Cause of Deafness.

| From What Disability. | No. | From What Disability. | No. |
|---|---|---|---|
| Concussion from artillery | 10 | Exposure from various causes | 12 |
| Exposure and catarrh | 14 | Bilious fever | 1 |
| Exposure after being wounded | 10 | Chills and fever and too much quinine | 4 |
| Exposure and chronic inflammation from middle ear | 1 | Explosion of shell | 10 |
| Typhoid fever and concussion | 1 | Gun-shot wound | 6 |
| Scurvy, exposure and sunstroke | 2 | Exposure and concussion | 4 |
| Concussion and injury | 4 | Typhoid fever and catarrh | 5 |
| Exposure and typhoid fever | 1 | Sunstroke | 4 |
| Exposure while in prison | 4 | Accident | 6 |
| | | Measles | 3 |

## TABLE 4.—Ages.

| Age. | No. | Age. | No. | Age | No. |
|---|---|---|---|---|---|
| 43 | 3 | 50 | 6 | 58 | 9 |
| 44 | 5 | 51 | 5 | 59 | 3 |
| 45 | 11 | 52 | 4 | 60 | 6 |
| 46 | 3 | 53 | 4 | 63 | 2 |
| 47 | 7 | 51 | 5 | 65 | 2 |
| 48 | 3 | 55 | 7 | 67 | 3 |
| 49 | 5 | 56 | 4 | 70 | 2 |

## TABLE 5.—From What State Enlisted.

| State. | No. | State. | No. |
|---|---|---|---|
| New York | 16 | Iowa | 10 |
| Michigan | 6 | Illinois | 12 |
| Nebraska | 4 | Pennsylvania | 6 |
| Virginia | 2 | Massachusetts | 2 |
| Minnesota | 4 | Vermont | 4 |
| Wisconsin | 5 | Rhode Island | 1 |
| Missouri | 5 | Connecticut | 2 |
| Ohio | 10 | New Hampshire | 1 |
| Indiana | 12 | | |

### Anomalies of Audition.

[Noises in the ear, false hearing, painful hearing, hallucinations, etc., to insanity and brain affections.]

Noises in the ears and head are nearly always present in some degree in both acute and chronic aural diseases, and a knowledge of their significance is necessary in arriving at a correct diagnosis.

The most common description of noises, imaginary songs and sounds of a soldier's life, and in the ear, is that of tinkling or tingling, "a tremulous jarring in the ears like ringing metal when struck," as the continuous vibration of a bell. They frequently remind the patient, however, of some familiar sound; thus the domestic fancies that they resemble the sound of frying food, boiling water, and the like: the rustic compares them to the agitation of leaves in the forest by the wind, or the singing of insects, etc.

The appended list of noises and other distressing anomalies are taken from these letters, and may be described as follows:

"Snapping noises," "sounds like distant thunder," "booming of artillery," "blowing or escaping of steam from an engine or locomotive," "blowing on mouth of bottle," blowing or scream of steam whistle," "clattering and buzzing to be heard in a planing mill," "a keen cracking sound like the report of a rifle, but much louder," "catching a severe cold causes a conglomeration of sounds that would defy competition, combined with a dozen other disagreeable noises thrown in," "sounds like some one striking an immense bell one stroke, the vibration distinctly heard until it dies away," "sounds like the falling of water from an elevation or cataract," "sounds like the old-fashioned spinning-wheel," "noises like millions of grasshoppers," "singing of crickets," "roaring sound like wild beasts," "cracking noises," "ringing of bells," "rumbling," "hissing of steam," "thunder," "dogs howling," "children crying," "men quarreling," "cannon booming," "humming or buzzing of saws," "music of organ," "sounds like thousands of imps talking and quarreling," "sounds like a train of cars running over a bridge," "ringing of steel plate," "striking an anvil," "sounds like some one singing old army songs," etc.

Some of the relations of certain aural phenomena are many and severe, memory impaired, nervous prostrations, great difficulty experienced after night in getting around, causing dizziness, with a staggering, stumbling, unsteady step, especially in stooping over, causes blindness, with an inclination to pitch forward, paralysis or numbness of feeling in the head, vertigo, loss of the senses of taste and smell, severe and acute pains in the head and ears, restless in sleep, depression of mind and body, susceptible to colds on the least change in the weather, which increases the disability, nervousness, nervous debility, stinging sensations in the ears, rushing of blood to the head, imperfect sight, loss of voice, headache, neuralgia, choking sensations while asleep, loss of memory, insomnia, distressing dreams, with many other irregularities that would sound unreasonable and impossible to those who have perfect hearing.

WALLACE FOSTER,
*Secretary and Treasurer*
*Silent Army of Deaf Soldiers, Sailors and Marines.*

INDIANAPOLIS, INDIANA, January, 1890.

## A DEAF SOLDIER'S DREAM.

DEDICATED TO MY COMRADES OF THE SILENT ARMY.

As I lay on my bed thinking of the many sufferings and ills of man, I insensibly fell asleep, and dreamed there was a proclamation issued by the "great reformers" that every mortal should bring in his disabilities and calamities and throw them together in a heap. There was a plane selected for this purpose, and I went with the rest, but being deaf and not able to hear what was said, I took a conspicuous stand and saw, with a degree of pleasure, the human species marching one after another and throwing down their several loads of infirmities, which immediately grew up into a mountain There was a certain reformer who was very active in the solemnity of the occasion, and led up every mortal to the appointed place and officially assisted him in disposing of his grievances. My heart melted within me to see my fellow-creatures groaning under their respective burdens, and to consider that prodigious bulk of human calamities which lay before me. There were multitudes with very whimsical burdens who, upon getting sight of the heap, shook their heads and went away as they came. I saw multitudes of old women throw down their wrinkles, and several young ones who divested themselves of a tawny skin. There were very great heaps of red noses, large, thick lips, rusty teeth, etc. Observing one advancing towards the heap with rather a peculiar gait, I found on his near approach that he was a soldier with a crutch, which he disposed of with a great deal of joy and satisfaction among this collection of human miseries and disabilities of all kinds. When the whole race of mankind had thus cast away their burdens, the reformer, who had been so busy on this occasion, seeing me an idle spectator of what passed, approached toward me. I grew uneasy at his presence, when, without ceremony, he began to talk to me, being able to catch the angry expression of his face and motion of his lips. I tried hard, but in vain, to catch his words, which made me very angry and out of humor with myself, upon which I threw my deafness in the heap. It happened that the one who stood nearest to me after I made my deposit was the one-legged soldier who had thrown down his crutch. This soldier and many others, when they saw me throw down my deafness, laughed, as if to say, "You are certainly a very foolish man to throw away as trifling a disability as deafness." The soldier learning I was a comrade of his, slipped me a note, advising me to take up my deafness, slip away and keep quiet; that I could not expect to better my condition in that crowd by an exchange, etc. I told him to "grab a root."

All the contributions being now in, we were told everyone was at liberty to exchange his misfortunes for those of any other person's on the heap. The hurry and confusion at this announcement could not be described. All of the observations, I upon the occasion saw, I could not communicate to others, but in the hurly, burly, grab game, the best I could do was to get the soldier's crutch, and he appeared content to get hold of my deafness. I could not but help notice he kept watching me with a sympathetic eye, expecting me to ask him to rue the trade. Not being disposed to incumber myself by talking to a deaf man I remained quiet, and was content to go with the throng to our respective homes. I soon lost sight of my deaf comrade, and on my way home I heard many sounds to attract my attention, and more than once misplaced my crutch and fell to the ground. The birds overhead appeared to be directing their sweet songs to attract my attention. The beautiful silvery waters, as they came rippling down the slope, caused me more than once to stop and listen. On my way home I came to a road, and by the wayside stood a pump. I halted for a drink and to refresh myself. While there a lady drove up to water her horse, and to show my gallantry I watered her horse; and as she started off, supposing me an object of charity, handed me twenty-five cents, and expressed a wish that I might ride by her side, which invitation I accepted. The horse ran away, tipping the cart over and throwing us on the ground, with a few bruises. But for the accident the ride was pleasant.

The cart being once more in position we rode on, and soon came to a fork in the road where we had to separate. Her parting words were, "There is nothing too good for our limbless soldiers," and she actually wanted to kiss me, but of course I told her that would not do, and I again resumed my crutch walk.

I soon arrived in the city, and stopping on the street corner to rest and get my breath, took off my hat to wipe the sweat from my brow. The passers-by took me for an object of charity and began dropping money in my hat. This was too embarrassing for me, so I placed my hat on my head, and just as I was adjusting my crutch under my arm preparatory to starting, a frisky Jew came around the corner, running square against me and dislocating my crutch. He was very kind, however, and stopped to help me and my crutch concentrate our forces.

Being once more in a perpendicular shape, I passed on, not, however, until the Jew handed me his business card, requesting me to call and receive a present in token of regret at his awkwardness. In passing on toward home there were many remarks that attracted my attention by persons who, seeing my G. A. R. badge, would say, "Poor fellow, he has left his leg on some Southern battle-field."

One good old lady, seeing I was weary, asked me to stop and take tea with her, and in sweetening my tea, insisted on making it too sweet for my taste. She had already put in one large spoonful of sorghum molasses, and insisted on putting in a second spoonful, saying there was nothing too good for wounded soldiers The hospitalities received from this kind old lady revived me, and I hobbled on toward my home. Not wanting to surprise my wife too suddenly and cause her trouble by thinking I had met with another misfortune, I appointed a committee from my neighborhood to break the news to her gradually, and inform her of my exchange, etc. While I was awaiting the report of the committee, thinking over the haps and mishaps of the day, my mind drifted to my deaf comrade and his distressed condition. I knew from my day's experience that I would soon become accustomed to my crutch, and be all the better qualified for business and social company, and consequently be less of a burden to myself and friends. Not so with my deaf comrade. I knew only too well that time would make his life more and more burdensome to himself and friends, and he would never become accustomed to deafness and its accompanying disadvantages. While I thus allowed my heart to go out in full sympathy for my poor deaf comrade, I heard the voices of a merry crowd, and looking up saw wife and committee coming toward me. As they approached I could see an expression of sadness in all their faces except my own good wife, who, knowing my former sufferings next to myself, saw at once the change could not be for the worse So on they came in double time. My wife being unaccustomed to the tricks of a crutch, and not stopping to consider (I was yet a raw recruit in the crutch drill), came at me with a front passade, which caused me to make a right rear vault, throwing my crutch somewhat in a semicircle to a fierce parry, but with my endeavors and her assistance I regained the position of guard, and was conducted home.

The neighbors gathered in and expressed themselves very freely as to the propriety of the exchange. My nearest neighbors were unanimous in the belief that it would be a great source of comfort, not only to myself and family, but to all my intimate friends and neighbors. Those who lived far away from me and knew but little of the displeasures of having a severely deaf neighbor, shook their heads in doubt, saying it was a terrible thing to go limping through this world on a crutch; but as the exchange was made, and there was no visible way of helping it, they advised me to not even think discouragingly, much worse feel so, for it would only make matters worse, and for me to dispel all gloomy thoughts, and they would, each and every one of them, regardless of political belief, unite in an effort to get me nominated and elected to some county office at the coming fall election One good old lady advised me to study for the ministry, and when I assured her I could at least attend church and derive some pleasure in listening to the preaching of the gospel, her face brightened up with a ray of light, and she thanked her God for the blessed privilege.

There were many suggestions made as to the different situations and occupations I would now be able and competent to fill on account of being able to hear, etc. After I had heard what the neighbors had to say, I thanked the committee for their services, and they retired. Many business men, to whom I had applied in the past days for work and situations, and who had put me off for the reason of my deafness, came to me or sent me word they would be only too glad to give me the situation I had asked for

My old boss, a harness maker, called and left a pressing request that I should come back to the shop and stay with him; that as I could now hear I would be of great help to him in his sales-room and bench, also; that he would be willing to increase my wages. He told me he did hope my sudden elevation in life would not cause me to go back on the craft of "waxies," and that I would have to be careful or they would drag me into politics. I assured him that by putting a leather band around my head it would serve two purposes—keeping my head from bursting and furnishing the smell of leather, to ever remind me I was once a common mechanic. In my dream I resolved to stay at home for a while and practice crutch-drill before going out on the street. To tell you what fun I and that crutch had would tax your patience too much. My wife, seated on the grass on my parade ground, with our dog by her side, would become so overjoyed with laughter she would frequently roll on the grass, and the dog, not knowing what to make of my actions, would grab my crutch in his mouth and pull it from me. Through all this fun with the crutch my mind would become serious at times, when I would think of my poor deaf comrade, and wonder what kind of amusement he was making for his poor wife and dog. While I sat thus meditating and resting myself my wife asks the question: "Don't you think that fellow will hunt you up for a rue?" My dream here appeared to take a jump; some months had passed away, fall had come, a political campaign had been gone through, and I, as a poor, one-legged soldier candidate, had been elected by a large majority to the office of county treasurer. I had qualified, and was ready to take charge of the office in two weeks. During the two weeks I had agreed to help the boys in the shop, as times were very busy with them. In a few days a letter came from my poor, deaf comrade, which read as follows:

Dear Comrade—Through long and earnest endeavors I have at last succeeded in finding your address and whereabouts. I write to you asking you to open your heart as a comrade in full sympathy with one who is traveling in a dark, gloomy woods in silence and distress. No one could have told me the sufferings and distress of a deaf man. The infirmity I am trying to endure, but I must give up; I can not endure this silent life. You, dear comrade, may have become accustomed to the disability, to an extent. Had you explained to me when the exchange was made, the many disagreeable symptoms accompanying deafness, I would have been far from giving up my crutch. Why, I have continual distressing sounds in my head day and night, growling, muttering, booming and roaring, like so many wild beasts of the field. Of nights I get very little sleep, with most distressing dreams. All sources of enjoyment are cut off. I can not endure this silence. To be condemned to this solitary life is gradually wearing me out. I am debarred from all social enjoyment, from conversation, speaking, sermons, lectures, etc. Business that I attended to before I gave up my crutch, is now an impossibility, as far as attending to it is concerned, and am indeed in a precarious condition. What I shall do I can not tell. I had no idea of the many obstacles that would be in my way to earn a support and get employment, and what a constant source of anxiety and distress of mind I would have to endure. The deafness not only makes me have distressing noises in my head, but causes nervousness and depression of the mental organs. I find I can not control my step in walking, I become dizzy and stagger—feel as though I was tilting to the front. The awkwardness of my appearance in society makes me but little better than a dummy, and the replies I give to inquiries causes many a tittering smile at my expense. I am a tax on patience and society. But why do I write thus to you, knowing, as I do, you are well qualified and competent to judge my feelings, and extend to me your full sympathy. So here comes the business and object of this letter. I want to exchange with you, return this deafness for the crutch, and by way of a compromise, I will say, since the war, most of the time, I have had a fat office, besides Uncle Sam has given me a good pension, which has not only made it possible for me to feed, clothe and educate my dear little children and make them fit members of society, but it has enabled me to lay up quite a snug little sum of money. Now, comrade, if money will be any inducement to you, I am willing to divide, and hereafter extend to you fraternity and charity. I will call to see you in a very few days and hope to effect an exchange.

In conclusion, I appeal to you for mercy in my miserable condition.

Yours, etc.,

RICHARD HOLT.

The few days passed in sadness at our home; things were in a muddle. I had a conference with my bondsmen, and they informed me, as a severe deaf man it would be impossible for me to fill the office to which I had been elected and give satisfaction to the people, and that as I had already qualified it would not do for me to take back the deafness.

The few days came. I was working at my bench, trying to forget the past, when I heard some one coming through the door crying, "Have mercy! have

mercy!" Looking up, there stood before me the poor, hollow-eyed, sunken-cheeked and emaciated form of the deaf soldier, crying in a most horrible tone: "Oh! for the sake of my happiness and for the memory of our soldier days, have mercy! have mercy!" Knowing it was useless to try to talk to him, I shook my head, and he continued in a more horrible tone than before: "Oh, hard heart, are you yet unmoved? It will drive me mad! it will drive me mad!" and with hands clutched in his hair, he fell dead. (And I awoke, etc.)

JAMES J. REAGIN,
Lieut. Co. G, 2d Regiment Iowa Infantry,
Hamburg, Iowa.

www.ingramcontent.com/pod-product-compliance
Lightning Source LLC
Chambersburg PA
CBHW031823090426
42739CB00008B/1385

* 9 7 8 3 3 3 7 1 7 5 6 8 9 *